Pat Kin

Undern

Bloomsbury Methuen Drama
An imprint of Bloomsbury Publishing Plc

B L O O M S B U R Y
LONDON • NEW DELHI • NEW YORK • SYDNEY

Bloomsbury Methuen Drama

An imprint of Bloomsbury Publishing Plc

Imprint previously known as Methuen Drama

50 Bedford Square	1385 Broadway
London	New York
WC1B 3DP	NY 10018
UK	USA

www.bloomsbury.com

BLOOMSBURY, METHUEN DRAMA and the Diana logo
are trademarks of Bloomsbury Publishing Plc

This playtext first published by Bloomsbury Methuen Drama 2015

British Library Cataloguing-in-Publication Data
A catalogue record for this book is available from the British Library

ISBN: PB: 978-1-4742-2891-6
ePub: 978-1-4742-2892-3
ePDF: 978-1-4742-2890-9

Library of Congress Cataloging-in-Publication Data
A catalog record for this book is available from the Library of Congress

Typeset by Country Setting, Kingsdown, Kent CT14 8ES
Printed and bound in Great Britain

fishamble
THE NEW PLAY COMPANY

Fishamble:
The New Play Company
presents

Underneath

by

Pat Kinevane

Fishamble is funded by the Arts Council,
Dublin City Council and Culture Ireland.

Baile Átha Cliath
Dublin City

Culture Ireland
Cultúr Éireann

Underneath by Pat Kinevane was first produced
by Fishamble: The New Play Company
in the Lime Tree Theatre, as part of
Limerick City of Culture, on 5 December 2014
with the following cast and production team.

Cast

Pat Kinevane

Production Team

Director	Jim Culleton
Producer	Marketa Dowling
Composer	Denis Clohessy
Costume Stylist	Catherine Condell
Costume Builder	Mariad Whisker
Choreography Adviser	Emma O'Kane
Graphic Designers	Ronan Nulty & Dan O'Neill at Publicis
Dramaturg	Gavin Kostick
Stage Manager & Photographer	Ger Blanch
Production Photographer	Pat Redmond
Video Promotion	Evan Flynn
PR	Sinead O'Doherty at Gerry Lundberg PR
Assistant Director	Orna O'Connor *

*Placement as part of Fishamble's
theatre company-in-association status at UCD

Underneath
runs for approximately 80 minutes with no interval

Director's Note

Pat Kinevane wrote his first play, *The Nun's Wood*, for Fishamble in 1998, followed by *The Plains of Enna* in 1999. In 2006, Fishamble produced Pat's first solo play, *Forgotten*, and this was followed in 2011 by his second solo play, *Silent*. In all his plays, Pat is fearless and brave in the way he tackles issues that are close to his heart, and this is matched by his wicked sense of humour and inventive theatricality.

When we embarked on the productions of *Forgotten* and *Silent*, we had no idea that they would tour, not just across Ireland, but throughout Europe, Australia and the US. There is something so truthful and full of passion in Pat's writing and performance that connects with people, no matter where they are from.

In 2013, Pat and Fishamble started developing his third solo play, *Underneath*, and we were delighted when Karl Wallace and Jo Mangan asked us to premiere it as part of Limerick City of Culture. Pat wanted to write about a woman from Cobh whose name we do not know, and whose life had been shaped by the disfigurement she received when she was struck by lightning as a girl. The play explores prejudice, beauty and how we treat people according to their appearance; it does this with all of the joy, anger, playfulness and power that we have come to expect from Pat's writing.

We are rehearsing at the moment, and Pat's portrayal of a woman who looks like a man is full of beautiful sensitivity and savage energy. I think she will have an impact on audiences that is just as strong as her predecessors: Flor, Dora, Gustus and Eucharia in *Forgotten*, and Tino McGoldrig in *Silent*. Pat is a pleasure to work with, as is the whole team, including Marketa Dowling, Gavin Kostick, Denis Clohessy, Ger Blanch, Orna O'Connor, Emma O'Kane and Catherine Condell, whose support has been invaluable.

I am so grateful to all the venues and festivals that have hosted Fishamble's productions of Pat's plays so far, and to our partners – the Arts Council, Dublin City Council, Culture Ireland, Irish Theatre Institute, Dublin Theatre Festival, the Irish Arts Center (New York), The Odyssey (Los Angeles), Dance Base (Edinburgh), Arts Projects Australia, Georganne Aldrich Heller and Aurora Nova – whose support has been instrumental in bringing this work to audiences.

I hope you enjoy *Underneath* and being part of the journey of this new play with us.

Jim Culleton (2014)

Pat Kinevane

is a native of Cobh, Co. Cork. He has worked as an actor in theatre, film, television and radio for 25 years. As a writer he completed his first full-length play, *The Nun's Wood*, in 1997, which won a BBC Stewart Parker Trust Award and was produced by Fishamble. Fishamble then produced his second play, *The Plains of Enna* (Dublin Theatre Festival, 1999). Pat wrote *The Death of Herod* for Mysteries 2000 at the SFX. In 2008 his piece *Evangeline Elsewhere* premiered in New York in the First Irish Festival. Pat has been touring since 2006 with his two solo pieces *Forgotten* (*Irish Times* Theatre Award nominee) and *Silent* (*Scotsman* Fringe First and *Herald* Angel Awards and *Brighton Argus* Angel Award), all produced by Fishamble. Both shows have been performed extensively throughout Ireland and in Paris, Prague, Romania, Bulgaria, Germany, Turkey, Switzerland, England, Scotland, Wales, Croatia, Serbia, Iceland, Finland, Melbourne, Perth, Washington DC, Boston, New York and Los Angeles. Pat is deeply grateful to be able to present *Underneath* and is humbly thankful to Fishamble for all their work and support.

Jim Culleton

is artistic director of Fishamble: The New Play Company for which he has directed award-winning productions that have toured throughout Ireland, UK, US, Canada, Australia and 12 European countries. Most recent productions for Fishamble are *Spinning* by Deirdre Kinahan, *Little Thing, Big Thing* by Donal O'Kelly, *Tiny Plays for Ireland 1 & 2* by 50 writers, *The Pride of Parnell Street* by Sebastian Barry, *The Bruising of Clouds* and *Noah and the Tower Flower* by Sean P. Maguire, *The Music of Ghost Light* by Joseph O'Connor, and *Turning Point* in association with ADI/VSA/Kennedy Center. He has previously directed Pat Kinevane's multi-award winning *Silent* and *Forgotten* for Fishamble, which have toured extensively. He has also directed for the Abbey, most recently *Bookworms* by Bernard Farrell and *Shush* by Elaine Murphy, as well as for 7:84 (Scotland), Project Arts Centre, Amharclann de hÍde, Amnesty International, Tinderbox, The Passion Machine, The Ark, Second Age, RTÉ Radio, the Belgrade, TNL Canada, Scotland's Ensemble @ Dundee Rep, Draíocht, Barnstorm, Roundabout, TCD School of Drama, Guna Nua, RTE lyric fm, Frontline Defenders, Irish Council for Bioethics, Origin (New York) and Woodpecker Productions/Gaiety. He is adjunct lecturer at TCD, and has taught for Notre Dame, NYU, the Lir, NUIM/GSA, and UCD. Current projects for Fishamble include a range of training, mentoring and development initiatives, and he will next direct a revival of *Little Thing, Big Thing* in Wales, France, Switzerland and Ireland, as well as a selection of *Tiny Plays for Ireland* for Vessel/ATF as part of the Sydney Festival.

Marketa Dowling

is the general manager and producer of Fishamble: The New Play
Company for which she has most recently produced *Spinning* by Deirdre
Kinahan (Dublin Theatre Festival), *Swing* by Steve Blount, Peter Daly,
Gavin Kostick and Janet Moran (Irish tour and New York, Paris and
Edinburgh), *Little Thing, Big Thing* by Donal O'Kelly (Irish tour), *Guaranteed!*
(Irish tour), *Tiny Plays for Ireland 1* and *2* by 50 writers (Project Arts
Centre, Dublin), *The Great Goat Bubble* by Julian Gough (Galway Arts
Festival), *The Wheelchair on My Face* by Sonya Kelly (Irish tour and to
Paris, Edinburgh and New York), *The End of the Road* by Gavin Kostick
(offsite in Temple Bar, Dublin), multi-award winning *Silent* by Pat Kinevane
(Irish tour and Europe, Australia and US), *Forgotten* by Pat Kinevane
(throughout Ireland and Europe and US), the multi-award-winning *The
Pride of Parnell Street* by Sebastian Barry (Irish tour, London, New Haven,
Paris and Wiesbaden), a reading of *My Name Is Rachel Corrie* (Dublin) in
association with Amnesty International, and co-produced and stage
directed *Rank* by Robert Massey (Dublin Theatre Festival and London).
Marketa's producing credits for The Performance Corporation include
Slattery's Sago Saga by Arthur Riordan, *Power Point* by Tom Swift,
Theatrical Espressos *KISS USA* and *GAA!* and the Irish premiere of the
multi-disciplinary piece *Cool Fresh Milk*. In 2010, Marketa also produced
The Performance Corporation's SPACE Production Award in association
with Absolut Fringe: *From the Heart* by Louise White and Kate Nic
Chonaonaigh, *True Enough!* by Making Strange and *Help Me! Help Me!*
by Priscilla Robinson.

Denis Clohessy

has composed music and designed sound for Fishamble: The New Play
Company's *Spinning, Strandline, The Pride of Parnell Street* and *Silent*. He
has produced work for theatre and dance with the Abbey Theatre, Gate
Theatre, Rough Magic, The Corn Exchange, Junk Ensemble and many
others. He won the *Irish Times* Irish Theatre Award for Best Design Sound
in 2011, was an associate artist with the Abbey in 2008 and was a
participant on Rough Magic's ADVANCE programme in 2012. He has also
composed extensively for film and television, including *The Land of the
Enlightened* (Fastnet Films), *The Irish Pub* (Atom Films), *His and Hers*
(Venom Film), *The Reluctant Revolutionary* (Underground Films) and the
television series *Limits of Liberty* (South Wind Blows) performed by the
RTÉ Concert Orchestra.

Catherine Condell

recently worked on *Silent* by Pat Kinevane for Fishamble: The New Play
Company, and *Payback!* by Maria McDermottroe and Marion O'Dwyer as
part of Show in a Bag. Catherine has worked in the fashion industry for

35 years, initially as a display artist and then as fashion stylist and fashion show producer. She worked for the Brown Thomas group for over 20 years and produced the Supermodel Shows in 1996, 2000 and 2003. She has worked with Naomi Campbell, Christy Turlington, Helena Christensen, Yasmin Le Bon, Eva Herzigova and Erin O'Connor.

Emma O'Kane

is a freelance dancer and choreographer. This is the first time she has worked with Fishamble. She has been a core member of CoisCeim Dance Theatre since 2001. Dance Europe voted Emma Outstanding Dancer of the Year for her performance in CoisCeim's production of *FAUN*. She was awarded Winner Best Female Actress for the ensemble cast of *Her Mother's Daughters* (a dance short, part of RTE's *Dance on the Box*). Recent choreography credits for dance, theatre and opera companies include *The Chilean Trilogy* (Prime Cut Productions), *The Sleeping Queen* (Wexford Festival Opera), *Farm*, *CARE* (Willfredd Theatre), *Angel Meadow, Laundry, Basin* (Anu Productions), *Four Told* (Project Arts Centre), *Solo Collective*, *O Mio Babbino Caro*, *Casta Diva*, *Padam Padam* and *La Goulante du Pauvre Jean* (CoisCéim Broadreach), *The Seagull* (NAYD), *At Peace* (Upstate Theatre), *The Crock of Gold* (Storytellers Theatre Company). Emma was assistant director on *A Midsummer Night's Dream* for Opera Ireland's Winter Season 2008 and *Macbecks* (Long Road Productions). In 2010, with Muirne Bloomer, she created and performed *The Ballet Ruse* supported by the Arts Council (Dance Project Award, Touring and Dissemination of Work Scheme). It was part of the Culture Ireland Showcase in Edinburgh 2011, nominated for Best Production at the Dublin Fringe Festival 2010 and shortlisted for a Total Theatre Award at the Edinburgh Festival Fringe.

Gavin Kostick

is literary officer at Fishamble: The New Play Company, working with new writers for theatre through script development for production, readings and a variety of mentorship programmes. Gavin is also an award-winning playwright who has written over twenty plays produced nationally and internationally. Recent works include *The End of the Road* for Fishamble, *This is What we Sang* for Kabosh (Belfast and New York), *The Sit* and *Fight Night* (on tour 2011) and *An Image for the Rose* outdoors for Whiplash Theatre Company. His latest work, *The Games People Play* for RISE Productions, has won the *Irish Times* Irish Theatre Award for Best New Play 2013. He wrote the libretto for *The Alma Fetish*, composed by Raymond Deane, which was staged in 2013 by Wide Open Opera at the National Concert Hall. As a performer, he performed Joseph Conrad's *Heart of Darkness: Complete,* a six-hour show for Absolut Fringe, Dublin Theatre Festival and the London Festival of Literature at Southbank.

**Fishamble wishes to thank
the following Friends of Fishamble
for their invaluable support**

Alan and Rosemarie Ashe, Mary Banotti, Tania Banotti,
Halsey and Sandra Beemer, Padraig Burns, Claudia Carroll,
Maura Connolly, Ray Dolphin, John Fanagan, Barbara FitzGerald,
Cora Fitzsimons, Brian Friel, Pauline Gibney, Ann Glynn,
John and Yvonne Healey, Eithne Healey, Georganne Aldrich Heller,
Gillie Hinds, Jane and Geoffrey Keating, Lisney, Liz Nugent
and Richard McCullough, Lucy Nugent, Patrick Molloy,
Aidan Murphy, Dympna Murray, Vincent O'Doherty, Joanna Parkes,
Nancy Pasley, David and Veronica Rowe, Colleen Savage,
Mary Sheerin, Grace Smith. Thank you to all
who do not wish to be credited.

Special thanks to: David Parnell, Maeve Giles and all at the Arts Council;
Ray Yeates and all at Dublin City Council Arts Office; Louise Donlon
and all at the Lime Tree Theatre, Karl Wallace, Jo Mangan,
Maeve McGrath, Mike Fitzpatrick, Sheila Deegan and all
at Limerick City of Culture, Andrea Cleary, Axis Ballymun,
Joe Flavin, Adam Fitzsimons, and all those who have helped
Fishamble with the production since this publication
went to print.

Fishamble Needs Your Support

Become a Friend of Fishamble today and support new theatre making
at its best, whilst enjoying the benefits of complimentary tickets,
discounts on playwriting courses and exclusive Friends events.

For further information see www.fishamble.com/support-us
or contact Marketa Dowling on
01 6704018

About Fishamble: The New Play Company

'Fishamble puts electricity in the National Grid of dreams'
Sebastian Barry

'Without Fishamble, Irish theatre would be anaemic'
Brian Friel

Fishamble is an award-winning, internationally acclaimed Irish theatre company dedicated to the discovery, development and production of new work. So far, it has produced 55 productions of new plays, including seven productions of multi-writer works, which included 89 short plays. Fishamble is committed to touring throughout Ireland and internationally, and typically presents over 200 performances of its plays in approximately 60 venues per year.

Fishamble has earned a reputation as 'a global brand with international theatrical presence' (*Irish Times*), 'forward-thinking Fishamble' (*New York Times*) and 'Ireland's excellent Fishamble' (*Guardian*) through touring its productions to audiences in Ireland as well as to England, Scotland, Wales, France, Germany, Iceland, Croatia, Belgium, Czech Republic, Switzerland, Bulgaria, Romania, Serbia, Turkey, Finland, USA, Canada and Australia.

Awards for Fishamble productions include Fringe First, Herald Angel, Argus Angel, MAMCA, 1st Irish and Irish Times Theatre Awards. Many of its first-time playwrights have won Stewart Parker Trust Awards. During 2013, to celebrate the company's 25th birthday, Fishamble donated its living archive to the National Library of Ireland.

Fishamble is at the heart of new writing for theatre in Ireland, not just through its productions, but through its extensive programme of training, development and mentoring schemes. Each year, Fishamble typically supports 60 per cent of the writers of all new plays produced on the island of Ireland, approximately 55 plays per year. This happens in a variety of ways; for instance, Fishamble supports:

- **the public** through an ongoing range of playwriting courses in Dublin and off-site for venues and festivals nationwide;

- **playwrights and theatre companies nationwide** through *The New Play Clinic*, which develops new plays planned for production by theatre artists and companies, and the annual *Fishamble New Writing Award* at Dublin Fringe;

- **actors** through its *Show in a Bag* programme, which creates and showcases new plays for actors, in association with the Irish Theatre Institute and Dublin Fringe;

- **students** through work in association with TCD, NUIG, NUIM, IES, DIT, through the inclusion of Fishamble plays on the secondary school English curriculum, and as *Theatre Company in Association* at UCD Drama Studies Centre;

- **emerging artists** through *Mentoring Schemes* in association with venues and local authorities for playwrights and directors.

New plays are under commission from Sebastian Barry, Gavin Kostick, Pat Kinevane, Darren Donohue, Colin Murphy, Deirdre Kinahan and Rosaleen McDonagh, as well as a project-in-development with CoisCeim and Crash Ensemble.

Fishamble Staff

Artistic Director	Jim Culleton
General Manager	Marketa Dowling
Literary Manager	Gavin Kostick

Fishamble Board

Tania Banotti, Padraig Burns, Peter Finnegan, Liz Nugent, Vincent O'Doherty, Andrew Parkes (Chair).

Fishamble: The New Play Company

Shamrock Chambers
1/2 Eustace Street
Dublin 2
Ireland

Tel: +353–1-670 4018, fax: +353–1-670 4019
E-mail: info@fishamble.com

www.fishamble.com
www.facebook.com/fishamble
www.twitter.com/fishamble

Previous Fishamble World Premiere Productions

2014
Spinning by Deirdre Kinahan
Little Thing, Big Thing by Donal O'Kelly
Silent by Pat Kinevane (revival)
Swing by Steve Blount*, Peter Daly*, Gavin Kostick and Janet Moran*
Forgotten by Pat Kinevane (revival)

2013
The Bruising of Clouds by Sean McLoughlin (now Sean P. Maguire)
Guaranteed! by Colin Murphy*
Tiny Plays for Ireland 2 by 25 writers
Silent by Pat Kinevane (revival)
The Great Goat Bubble by Julian Gough (revival)
The Wheelchair on My Face by Sonya Kelly (revival)
Forgotten by Pat Kinevane (revival)

2012
Tiny Plays for Ireland by 25 writers
Silent by Pat Kinevane (revival)
The Great Goat Bubble by Julian Gough*
The Wheelchair on My Face by Sonya Kelly*
Forgotten by Pat Kinevane (revival)

2011
Silent by Pat Kinevane
The End of the Road by Gavin Kostick
The Pride of Parnell Street by Sebastian Barry (revival)
Forgotten by Pat Kinevane (revival)
The Music of Ghost Light by Joseph O'Connor
Noah and the Tower Flower by Sean McLoughlin (revival)

2010
Big Ole Piece of Cake by Sean McLoughlin
Turning Point by John Austin Connolly, Steve Daunt*, Stephen Kennedy,
Rosaleen McDonagh
Forgotten (revival) by Pat Kinevane

2009
Strandline by Abbie Spallen
The Pride of Parnell Street by Sebastian Barry (revival)
Forgotten by Pat Kinevane (revival)
Handel's Crossing by Joseph O'Connor
Noah and the Tower Flower by Sean McLoughlin (revival)

2008

Forgotten by Pat Kinevane (revival)
The Pride of Parnell Street by Sebastian Barry (revival)
Rank by Robert Massey

2007

The Pride of Parnell Street by Sebastian Barry
Noah and the Tower Flower by Sean McLoughlin*
Forgotten by Pat Kinevane

2006

Monged by Gary Duggan (revival)
Whereabouts – a series of short, site-specific plays
by Shane Carr*, John Cronin*,
John Grogan*, Louise Lowe, Belinda McKeon*,
Colin Murphy*, Anna Newell*,
Jack Olohan*, Jody O'Neill*, Tom Swift and
Jacqueline Strawbridge*
The Gist of It by Rodney Lee*

2005

Monged by Gary Duggan*
She Was Wearing ... by Sebastian Barry, Maeve Binchy,
Dermot Bolger, Michael Collins,
Stella Feehily, Rosalind Haslett, Róisín Ingle*,
Marian Keyes* and Gavin Kostick

2004

Pilgrims in the Park by Jim O'Hanlon
Tadhg Stray Wandered In by Michael Collins

2003

Handel's Crossing by Joseph O'Connor,
The Medusa by Gavin Kostick, *Chaste Diana*
by Michael West and *Sweet Bitter* by Stella Feehily
(a season of radio plays)
Shorts by Dawn Bradfield*, Aino Dubrawsky*,
Simon O'Gorman*, Ciara Considine*,
Tina Reilly*, Mary Portser, Colm Maher*,
James Heaney*, Tara Dairman*,
Lorraine McArdle*, Talaya Delaney*, Ger Gleeson*,
Stella Feehily* and Bryan Delaney*
The Buddhist of Castleknock by Jim O'Hanlon (revival)

2002

Contact by Jeff Pitcher and Gavin Kostick
The Buddhist of Castleknock by Jim O'Hanlon*
Still by Rosalind Haslett*

2001
The Carnival King by Ian Kilroy*
Wired to the Moon by Maeve Binchy, adapted by Jim Culleton

2000
Y2K Festival: Consenting Adults by Dermot Bolger,
Dreamframe by Deirdre Hines,
Moonlight and Music by Jennifer Johnston,
The Great Jubilee by Nicholas Kelly*,
Doom Raider by Gavin Kostick, *Tea Set* by Gina Moxley

1999
The Plains of Enna by Pat Kinevane
True Believers by Joseph O'Connor

1998
The Nun's Wood by Pat Kinevane*

1997
From Both Hips by Mark O'Rowe*

1996
The Flesh Addict by Gavin Kostick

1995
Sardines by Michael West
Red Roses and Petrol by Joseph O'Connor*

1994
Jack Ketch's Gallows Jig by Gavin Kostick

1993
Buffalo Bill Has Gone To Alaska by Colin Teevan
The Ash Fire by Gavin Kostick (revival)

1992
The Ash Fire by Gavin Kostick*
The Tender Trap by Michael West

1991
Howling Moons/Silent Sons by Deirdre Hines*
This Love Thing by Marina Carr

1990
Don Juan by Michael West

* denotes first play by a new playwright as part of Fishamble Firsts

Author's Thanks

My mother, Marie, my late father Denis and brother Alan, my sisters, Betty and Julie, my brothers, John, Denis and Mattie, my late aunt, Teresa O Rourke, and all of my extended family. Big thanks and huge love to Fionnuala Murphy, Kez Kinevane, Claudia Carroll, Frank Mackey, Fiona Lalor, Marion O'Dwyer, Catherine Condell, Ger Blanch, Denis Clohessy, Clodagh O'Donoghue, Amelia Crowley, Anthony Brophy, Anne Layde, Claire Cullinane, Noreen Brennan, Clelia Murphy, Conor and Maria McDermottroe, Fiona Condon, Lt. Comm Liam Smith (RIP), Joan O Hara (RIP), Des Cave, John Olohan, Maire Hastings and Andy O Ghallichor (RIP), Helen Norton, Marion McAuliffe, Siobhan Miley (RIP), Georganne Aldrich Heller and Norman Sachs, Noelle Brown, Olwen Fouere, Rachael Rogers, Sinead Keenan and Stefan Buttner, Niall Toner, Caitriona Ni Mhurchu, Liza Moynihan, Dessie Gallagher, Malachy McKenna, Brian Roche, Fergal Murphy, and all dearest friends for their constant care and support. I love you all so very much.

Author's Note

Underneath took me by surprise. In 2011, I began to think about words. Words have always fascinated me and more so when they are formed and released from the mouth. How joyful they can be, how hollow, how cruel. I thought of how different things said to me throughout my life have affected my self-esteem. Comments about my work, my personality, my body or my face. I realised during this time of reflection that the power of uplifting or brutal words was akin to throwing, or not throwing, a grenade. The responsibility is huge – we all must be enormously careful and delicate when commenting on others . . . as some words send vicious shrapnel to the bone. I was curious also about the growing disease of perfection that is epidemic on our planet. I have always found perfection in the asymmetric and flawed – that is my idea of pure beauty, a beauty that depends on the unbeautiful to compare and contrast itself to. In this way, a new balance is formed, in each of us, and we discover that our so-called flaws are actually our strengths and treasures. They are what makes each of us unique and perfect . . . because perfection, surely, is whatever brings us, individually, to our own personal completion. And Death as a concept arrived beside these musings on Cruelty and Beauty – I then understood fully the power of decay . . . that the husk of our bodies is just that . . . a kind host to what is the real person, the real spirit, a husk that houses the Soul. Some husks find another to go through life with. Some don't. So, Loneliness was my fourth slice of the pizza of my thoughts. I made the dough, rolled it out, threw all the toppings in the air – Cruelty, Beauty, Death and Loneliness – and they landed and cooked together. I hope that audiences enjoy even the tiniest bite. After all, I can't second guess their taste. I honestly can never imagine what I can fully do to surprise them, Underneath!

Working on all three solo pieces has been a humbling pleasure. Jim Culleton, Marketa Dowling, Orla Flanagan and Gavin Kostick at Fishamble have been extraordinary to work with.

They have nurtured and protected me, constantly. Jim has a serene energy which bathes and swaddles every word of a script. He cares deeply for the intent, thoughts and efforts of the writer. He is gifted to deal with my ups and downs and madness. He is a beautifully patient and creative director – devoid of ego and negativity. I have felt safe to fly to the crazy places in my world with him by my side as a writer and performer. He takes my fear away and reminds me of my playfulness and glee. He is a consummate professional and stunning creator of a theatrical event. I would have stopped both writing and acting years ago if it were not for his compassion and belief in me.

My passion for theatre began at five years old. I have no history or connections with the arts in my family whatsoever. I always knew that the theatre was where I felt safe and strong – where I felt I could say what my heart yearned to express. I still feel this at forty-eight years old and am steely in my conviction that the theatre is a place for all, from all backgrounds and circumstances. Theatre should not be the property of the elite or those in the know – it should not be analysed by academia to the point of utter deconstruction. It should be available to all, speak to all, mirror all.

I am overwhelmed with gratitude to anyone who ever helped or encouraged me to do my work. I am forever thankful.

Pat Kinevane, 2014

Underneath

for my eternal friend Frank Mackey
and
in memory of my loving and beautiful brother, Alan

Characters

Her

The solo performer also conjures every other role.

Setting

The setting is a black area.

There is a black, raised slab centre stage. Upstage right hangs a magnificent golden length of fabric. Another length drapes over the slab. Downstage left hangs an opulent golden scarf, needles and wool.

Scattered about the space are a golden magazine, a golden lampshade, a golden wallpaper roll, a golden tea towel, a golden glove and two golden J-cloths.

Notes

'Call and Answer' is a musical duet of lament and passion.

When Jasper is seen he wears the golden lampshade as a crown.

A 'soul-sucking moment' is a whipping assault on the senses.

The foxes scratching are always uncomfortably close.

And so the sound of a gentle harp . . . languid . . . and then another, and another overlapping that, and then wind, and more harps and distant strings, and then further wind and more layered harps, passing birds of prey and the distant barks of foxes, then . . . growing strings and then bigger wind and an eastern voice from an ancient place, and the pace increases and the coming and going of a man's call, a song or sound of pleading, and the harps ripple and the wind is getting faster and the overture is becoming frantic and the birds call and on and on it all overlaps together, faster and gasping, all gets frantic and sucking us in – like a helicopter, whipping us up and swirling us as we fall around the sky of the desert . . . and then land and . . . we come upon a figure in jet black and grey. All that shows are its teeth and the fantastic whites of its eyes. Its face is stained with gold. Then . . . words are spoken . . .

Her   You never know what's around the corner, do ya? (*A smile.*)

You're all very welcome. Catch your breath there and we'll chat in a minute!

Call and Answer.

So, the Tumbledown Cemetery, Cobh, County Cork . . . am . . . the chapel ruins are over that way, we are in the ground west of the nave, surrounded by the old gentry and clergy. The tombs are lined with slate and the slabs on top are solid granite, some broken. Ours is intact with teensy cracks that let the slivers of light in. One of Napoleon's doctors, actually, is in a vault over that way. Don't worry . . . there's no rats in this part but there's a fox family in the grave next door and I'm here since the night of the black smoke from the green bin and white smoke for Francis the First on the thirteenth of the third 'thirteen!

Now picture this. Wembley Stadium. Eighty thousand mixed crowd. On stage, the Queen and the Pope. She says, 'With one small gesture of one's hand one can make so many British go wild.' And she does this. They go 'Waaaaa'. He says, 'With one small movement of my head, I can make all the Irish go crazy.' And he headbutts her!

So, before the maggots, I lived in a flat near Croke Park in Dublin. I lived on the first floor and two hookers lived upstairs. I'd spent fifteen years there, alone, and nobody really knew that much about me because, well, they never asked and because . . . well, I chose to be private. I worked nights mostly in a hotel off Baggot Street . . . on the late bar and prepin' breakfast till dawn. Outside that, I spent all of my time indoors. The rent was low, my bike was in the hall . . . it was my safe and cosy nest. And when the Gardaí cordoned it off, it was spotless and not a trace of blood or fingerprints to be found . . . only a pizza receipt. But I am back in my home town now, and there isn't a decent soul knows where I am . . . so that's why I really appreciate your company . . . Thanks a tousand.

Call and Answer.

Ye never know what's round the corner, do ya? And when ya get that – 'understand the concept' as they say – it makes the shock of surprises easier to get over. What is around the corner?

A question for one of the audience perhaps.

Well the only person who had an answer to that was the slowest man down south . . . Galapagos. He spent twenty hours day and night, walking the roads of Cobh as if moving through treacle and he ranting to himself, 'Loadsa tings, loadsa tings,' and the lads would wind him up as he snailed along and say . . . 'Galapagos, C'm'ere, Galapagos! What's around the corner?' And the tortoise would reply . . . 'Loadsa tings . . . Small country . . . I'm tellin' the guards' . . . and he would, he told them everything, every evenin' at ten sharp . . . what he saw, who he passed, how many cars went by and the exact reg. of each . . . he had the cops tormented . . . but they had to listen . . . cos he had the right to report what he witnessed! Good or bad.

How are ya feelin'?

(*An honest fact.*) Well . . . I have never felt so happy, ever. I have never felt so safe. Since I came across. And this chamber . . . about the size of me bathroom. Three hundred years ago I wouldn't have had a chance of burial in this section of the wormyard. This is definitely the haughty part . . . I'll put ye straight now, on the location. Cobh sits on the second biggest natural harbour in the world and was the last port of the Titanic before the big glug-glug . . . So that's where we are . . . Location, location, or a place in the sun!

Television   Sofie and Trevor have a budget of £560,000. They have been hunting for their dream home for twenty-seven years and are very particular about what they want. We are showing them possible options for a home across the foam, in the south of France.

Trevor   Kel grand enchantemant! It's an old barn conversion with exposed beams. Looks like it used to be a slaughterhouse, the butcher hooks stuck in the plaster are still a pretty feature . . . perhaps a hanging area for garlic or booquet garni! It's got lots of potential. Oooo laaaa laaa! What do you think, Sofie?

Her (*knitting*)   I was born on the day after my mother saw *Cleopatra* in 1965 but she didn't call me after Liz Taylor cos there was a ton of scandal about her and Richard Burton but if I was a boy she said she would have definitely called me Nile, after all things Egyptian, Nile O'Sullivan. I was a tall little girl, always. I had angular wide shoulders. Mam told me to be proud of them, like Joan Crawford was, and she was a Fla. So that comforted me, at the golden age of seven and me dwarfin' all the other lassies in my communion frock that Mam made from loads of remnants she collected. She dress-made and knitted for extra money. Daddy was a council worker. He used to try and kiss her but she'd always mop the lino. Now her brother, Uncle Blaise, was my favourite and he sang in the all-male choir. He'd sing to me when he would visit too and I loved when he'd pinch my cheeks . . .

Blaise   'Oh girl, how excellent, how excellent, is thy face . . .
youuu are the bestest girl, my bestest girl . . . in the world.'

Loud scratching sound.

Her   Listen . . . that's the foxes! They wrecked the skeleton
of the woman next door. Only her skull left. And a spine. I
calls her Victoria Beckham. V.B., ye alright, girl? Hasn't
eaten in years. Musta passed out!

Are ya ready? Set? Let's go . . .

Egyptian tones in the distance . . . Ghostly movement to accompany . . .

I was nine. Mam was at work cleaning the big houses on the
high road . . . shining rosewood and brass. This day, I went
picking periwinkles with an enamel bucket . . . cos I was out
of third class with a pretend toothache . . . She could check
on me out the bay windows. Up to this point in my tiny life,
nothing special had ever happened to me. Nothing. Oh,
except for Daddy leaving. Vanished . . . Out of the blue!
Now, it was just me and Mam and Pharaoh the cat who lived
in the coal shed and never came out and all you could see was
the whites of his eyes and his teeth. So I hopped from rock to
rock that morning in March and the mist was light and the
rumbles of thunder were no cause for concern . Alone but not
lonely and I was thinkin' of Uncle Blaise when he waved at me
from the choir the Sunday just past. His voice was mahogany
in my head . . . but then a sudden downpour so I ran up from
the water to shelter under the cypresses, and wallop! Bucket
explodes to pieces, me blown up into the air, slam on the
footpath, face burning – I could see the flames with my good
eye. I roared . . . and soaking showers, getting soggier like the
pain . . . and then my vision was above me and I could see
myself from twenty feet in the air, eyes so wide open . . .
staring and I felt absolutely no fear. My dead grandfather
appeared to me, and did this . . . (*Gestures.*) Then suddenly
I fell back down into my eyes as rapid as the rain and STOP!
I heard the sauntering Galapagos . . . faint . . . 'Loadsa
tings . . . Small country!' . . . Along he came, at a glacier pace.

If he had been faster, he could have raised the alarm and got me to the hospital earlier, and the damage might not have been as dreadful.

Then with extreme naturalism . . .

These eyelids almost welded together with the heat. This ear melted lower than the other. Burgundy scarring all along here and down my neck . . . Paralysed for a while. Terrible stammer. Could barely swallow, branchy marks all over this shoulder and arm. I was in hospital for three years in and out . . . Slow progress . . . until I started secondary school . . . mixed and ran by the brothers and the nuns . . . and then the oogling and pointing proper started. I was even more taller than the others now on top of things. I was broader and masculine and I will never know if that was because of the lightning interfering with my system or something . . . but my hearing was amazingly sharp – like an owl. But sure, you never know what's round the corner, do ya?

Television   Hello, everybody! We join Sofie and Trevor at house number two . . . in Espanya, por favor! . . . Trevor is confused . . .

Trevor   Aw, I like the inside, but I like the outside as well. It's very empty, but that's smashing because there's lots of space. It's really Spanish . . . I like the tiles everywhere . . . really Spanish . . . Which is lovlay! But it's got no windows whatsoever, which is strange! I'm slightly confused! Do you like it, Sofie?

Her   Now the teenage years are hard enough God knows, but to be beautiful must make it triple easier for a boy or a girl. Most presumed at the start, when I stuttered and my eyes rolled, that I was, empty, like an auld kettle in a summer ditch. And that affected my temper. Which I kept inside with all my strength. Ah, but I heard the insults – behind chestnut doors even – that I was spastic, simple, retarded . . . oh, and the best ever from Winnie Mattress, the school slut.

Winnie   Mashed-up monsterface mangirl.

Her   And a classic from me history teacher . . . Lispy
Langford . . .

Lispy   She'd be better off if that lightning killed her stone
dead!

Her (*with held fury*)   Lispy, don't ya think I thought that too?

Lispy   She'd be better off if that lightning killed her stone
dead!

Her   I heard him whisper way down the corridor. Then
walked toward him. He knew he was caught. And I said . . .

'Mr Langford, would ya like a glass of water . . . so you can
wash down your fuckin' foot!'

Call and Answer.

Sorry 'bout that . . . It's mad that ye're here with me. In
Cobh. I always felt like I was born on the brink of the world.
That I was near the cliffs of death, always. And here I am!
This place of, sort of, whipping energy. So close to ye, but,
cos of death, torn asunder.

(*Knitting.*) So, the girls who lived upstairs. Anka was thirty-four
and from Bulgaria . . . Barkin' mad, and when she got
homesick she would play the harp. Virtuoso. That was all she
had brought from home, 'bout that high and made of oak.
Any time day or night she would strike up. Lidia was Polish
and nearly forty and as well as shenanigans she was a lap
dancer and made great money. Lethal sense of humour, she
told me this the morning I last saw her: 'Why did the Polish
fella cross the road? Because he took the chicken's job!' They
were both amazing girls. Anka and Lidia. I called them Aldi
and Lidl! Great value, unbeatable prices . . . for the way we
live today!

Ye see at school – didn't make friends. Terrified. Didn't trust
anyone in case they were talkin' to me out of pity . . . and the
gorgeous girls. Shur every time I tried to ignore their beauty
I was reminded of the lack of mine. So embarrassed . . . and

the more I'd blush, the more my crusty stain would stand out. I was the junior Wimbledon fucking Champion at dodging mirrors.

Oh yeah, upstairs . . . Where are me J-cloths? The flat. It was vacant for my first six months. Then one day in August I heard the girls chatting through the ceilin'. Knew they were foreign. And after a month I copped on to the story. The only loudness was the odd time they would play music while they got ready for the men. Some called by day, most at night. But all very quiet and discreet . . . fellas from business or culchies up for a GAA match, or husbands bullied by their wives. Honest!

Then one Friday night I heard screamin' on the landing. Opened me door . . . Some brute bastard had Aldi pinned against the banister. I could taste her pain as he bate her. So a lifetime of fizz burst out of my bottle and I snapped and went apeshit . . . pounced like a panther on the fucker. Size a' me! He spat at me, kept spittin' like an asp. I dug my nails into his papyrus face. Kicked him in the balls and he buckled like a punctured bouncy castle. I stood on his head and let my whole body weight crush him into a beggin' sissy, pleadin' with me to please stop. Coughing mad . . . 'I am sorry, I am sorry, I am sorry!' The girls pulled me off him . . . He rolled down the stairs and out the door like a bead of mercury . . . shoutin' up at me, 'Ya ugly fuckin' madra . . . I'll be back to get ya, bitch, I'll fuckin' kill ya . . . I'll slice ya up ya horrible-lookin' cunt.'

Girls cleaned my face with redpoppy soap and washed and dried my hair. I slagged them and said I knew they were prossies cos when I spotted the clothes horse all the labels on their knickers said 'Next'! Best friends after that!

Supernatural observation here – fast and urgent. Glove on – big breath in!

I have a message coming through here for a man called Colm, or Colin or . . . Conny . . . anyhow, your mother is really upset and she says you're to check beneath your fourteen-year-old's bed cos the flies are from the food he keeps hiding

like the scrawny ribs under his Abercrombie T-shirt and
when that seagull flew into your double duvet on the line last
week, that was a signal from her over here . . . and if you
don't sort things she is gonna visit ya one of these nights . . .
at the end of your bed . . . and frighten the shit out of ya! I'm
back. Whew!

I was fifteen . . . just about coping with my, disability, as they
called it. And I hated that word because there was so much
I was able to do . . . It was others who disabled me – stickin'
kick-me signs and compasses in me back – that exhausted
me . . . And Mammy. She never stopped cleaning the house.
Even in the middle of the night. And she had wallpapered the
hall seven times that year already and each time I had to help
her hold the roll! I was an expert at it. My fits were less and
I had absolutely no problems with the study, just the usual
cruel laughter. But in a crocodile twist of fate, the attention
was taken off me by the arrival of my opposite . . . a stunning
young man, as if dropped by the Gods. Jasper Wade.

We do not see him but the lampshade is addressed . . .

Super-intelligent, but . . . He'd been expelled from loads of
boarding schools cos he was pure trouble. Our college was
the last resort. His father was a huge landowner – estate in
the family since the penal laws. He was the huntmaster of the
Island and had his antique dealership all over Munster. And
even though ours was a Catholic school, the nuns said yes to
his son. From that moment on, there were massive icebergs
ahead.

Soul-sucking moment of sound and light . . .

I should have warned ya, sorry. It's alright though. Nothing
sinister. Just a soul going to birth. Ye get used to it. But . . .
I don't care, the best invention to combat loneliness is the
box in the corner . . . And my bible was the RTE guide. Kept
hundreds of them stacked up by me window. Grand seat
actually. RTE, supportin' me arse! I avoided makeover
programmes like the plague . . . Most of the poor cows looked

worse after they got it done and . . . Fashion slots . . . God
help us! . . . 'Thanks for having me on and we have the loads
of the looks for the classy lady . . . First out we have Sarah
Jessica . . . she's a size two and is petrified since she was
removed from a gypsy camp for being so blond so she is
wearing a Chanel bag over her head which is all the rage . . .
it's a very period piece, and I call this look "Pride and
Petrified" and you can dress it up or dress it down with these
Edwardian fuck-me shoes from Penny's or a perspex thong so
you can show off your fanny!'

More loud scratching . . .

They have a mouse. Yeah, they're tossin' and scoffin' field
mice. Y'see I like to come back here often . . . to visit myself –
in my sleeping place, and pick up the odd stitch and merge in
and out of myself, in and out of my voice, my bones . . . and
I realise now that my body was just a shell, a kind host – it
was never me. Just a loyal vessel. I should have cared less and
laughed more.

I'd seen Jasper a week before he started in our school. Mam
was cleaning the lawn tennis club. I was helpin' her out with
the toilets and the kitchen. This day, he appeared – star
player for his ex-college. Now back to conquer the home
tournament. I heard the posh wans through the changing-
room walls – the original desperate housewives – whisperin'
filthy about his loins. Taking bets on the size of his prick, and
who would be the first to measure it! Yeah! They must have
been twice his age but every lady member lusted after his!

*Sound of a distant tennis-match shouts from an umpire: 'Net', 'First
service', 'Out' etc . . . We see him fully for the first time . . .*

He was like a Merchant fuckin' Ivory movie – quarried from
an alabaster mountain . . . heart-stoppingly hypnotic on the
court . . . focused on the ball like a handsome falcon . . . racing
the pace of all the pulses watching his wings. Under his spell.
Arctic-white hair pouring from his head. A sweatband like a
diadem for his brow. The curve of his back. The power of his

thighs. The wet of his lips. And then, one day, he walked past me pouring perspiration . . . and smiled. Why me from him? I was the ugliest. Was it pity? Or compassion for me, the girl blown apart, or was it, no!

He disappears.

Impossible ya stupid girl, ya fuckin' stupid girl. And that night I thumped myself across the face with a homework book and *La France en Direct* really hurt but I deserved it cos I was a stupid ugly girl.

State of me! Look at the state of me. This is how I landed. By the way, anything with me here was thrown in too, the lampshade, curtains 'n' stuff, cos they were spattered in blood. My skin turned like charcoal leather after only two weeks . . . Two weeks after that it turned as black as the fur on the back of a lion's ears. It's amazing how fast we decompose once the heat of the heart is gone. 'Near, far, wherever, ooooaaaaa . . . ' My last night at work was an engagement party, residents' bar. She showin' off her sparkler pissed on jagerbombs and up on a table singin' 'Near far ooooo' serenadin' her fiancé, then slips, arse over tit and bang . . . bursts her jaw and husband-to-be panics and races to the front desk for help but wrong turn and slams into a fish tank and smashes his nose passes out nee-naw nee-naw the happy couple carted off in an ambulance! All they were short was lifeboats, Morse code and Kate Winslet and they would have won an Oscar. 'Will go on an' onnnnnn!'

I used to walk the quietest way to school – down the hill, and past the stable walls – but this morning I bumped straight into him by the Honeysuckle Cottages. He had shorts on. Panting. I was mortified.

There is a strange undertone to his voice . . . we don't see him . . . She speaks live . . .

Jasper   Hello there.

Her   Hello.

Jasper Jasper.

Her Hello.

Jasper And you –

Her *stammers.*

Jasper I'll call you 'you'! Hello 'you'. Met you last week.
Remember?

Her Am, oh yeah.

Jasper Semi-final next week. Training hard.

Her You're very dedicated.

Jasper Thank you! Need some brekky now. I can smell the
coffee!

Her Oh?

Jasper Live just there at the end of the lane . . .

Her Ohh . . . the big

Jasper Yip. Wuthering Heights!

Her That's a palace. Mother o' God!

Jasper Ohhhh ! I'm Frisbeetarian . . .

Her What's that?

Jasper Well, us Frisbeetarians believe that after death, the
soul flies up on to the roof and stays there for eternity!

Her I laughed with him, and felt safe with him. I'd never
really felt safe around a man or a boy before . . . except for
Uncle Blaise. Him and Aunty Dolores couldn't have children.
But they always looked out for me. They were devoted to
each other . . .

*A small choral sample: 'Oh Lord . . . how excellent'. One minute. We
see Uncle Blaise at a given time, waving to her . . .*

I watched lovers for years passing by . . . and each time my heart would shudder with loneliness . . . knowing that I would never have a partner . . . that nobody would ever desire me, ever dissolve me with that all-dissolving love . . . Please, never let another go by you without a greeting, even an invisible one . . . Think them happiness, send them warmth from your deepest core, because they just might be feeling so alone and starving for contact with another of their species.

Sudden loud, urgent scratching . . .

They must have caught a bird. They always go crazy when it's a bird . . . Feathers everwhere! Like the weddings . . . The hotel turns into a zoo for fashionistas. I spy them arriving at the receptions – the Paris Hilton Cinderellas, who worship Brown Thomas and Lebeutin shoes, embalmed in make-up, and their lofty Jock boyfriends reekin' of Eau de Tom Ford and the night creeps in and so does the drink and the drugs and then the dollies disintegrate before my very eyes. I'm really well-balanced, me . . . I have a chip on both shoulders! But after midnight these girls are the real Kardashian knackers, who vomit in the flowerpots and piss in the lift!

One particular Jock boyfriend while back clickin' at me, 'Hey you, you there, Angelina Jolie, ha ha! Angelina ha ha! Five Mohitos here soon as and, ha ha! I am taking a selfie to prove I met Brad's wife, ha ha!'

So I says 'Sir, could I have a word in private, please?'

Jock   'I'd looooove that, Angie!'

Her   'Am, Sir, I reeeecooooogggggniseeee your voice.'

Jock   'What the ffffuck. Who are you?'

Her   'Am, an hour ago. I was delivering room service to the suite opposite the honeymoon one.'

Jock   'So.'

Her   'I heard you fuckin' the groom. I also heard ye both swear that ye'd never tell a soul ever.

'Now I won't tell the bride over there, if you promise not to mock me any more tonight, OK? Oh and the Mohitos? See your iPhone 5? Just text 1800 I will in my hole! Enjoy your stay!'

I kept my temper!

Knitting

My temper? My father. The constant question: 'How could he just leave me behind?' Auntie Dolores got elephants drunk at Mam's funeral. Told me that the parish priest made Dad marry Mam cos she was up the pole with me and if he didn't that she would be sent off to a convent up the country. I'm convinced he had a premonition that I would be damaged – maybe he couldn't handle that – so he left me behind? Behind to battle against the obsession with fascist perfection every day . . . gestapo girls who try to trip me on escalators and kick my back wheel, nazi ladies who march straight through me and skip queues, master-race lads and women who believe they have the God-given third-reich to treat me like a pigdog, because they are attractive on the outside. . . and I am not.

Call and Answer.

When I would fit, my neck would do this. Mostly happened in school. I would freeze. One minute of savage pain . . . then gone. Completely disorientated. And nobody ever gave me help. I think it just revolted everyone and they backed off. I had a whopper one in German class. They all left after the bell. Teacher as well, bollocks! But . . . Jasper stayed.

We see him for the second time.

Sat beside me for an hour . . . shushed away anyone who tried to interrupt. He asked me lotsa questions . . . to bring me back, to relax me I suppose . . .

Jasper   What's the scariest movie yev ever seen?

Who's your favourite member of Duran Duran?

Why do dogs do this when you ask them a question?

Her   And one question that I will never forget . . .

Jasper   When was the last time you felt pretty?

Her   And Downton fuckin' Abbey! And Dame Maggie as
the Dowager . . . with a mouth like a poodle's arsehole! Who
gives a shit about the day-to-day problems of the megawealthy
in their humongous house? Why does this fascinate people?
Frocks galore with their spinach moose and in this week's
episode . . . the son and heir of everything ponders: 'Dear
sweet one, shall I go to war, and miss your kiss, or ought I
remain here, and sip your piss! Carson, pour the wine. I feel
an alteration. A flux. Everything is changing, at Downton.'
Who gives a shit? And as for the servants downstairs
complainin' . . . 'By gum, my hands is down to the bone from
all that scrubbin' – every time a bell rings Daisy's got to doo
things' – get over it! You're a servant, serve! We should have
a whip-round here, right – put a goody parcel together full of
ropes, arsenic and semtex, post it care of 'The Big House' so
they can top themselves if it all gets too dramatic and
miserable! God help us!

But I did answer Jasper. The only time I felt anywhere close
to the land of pretty was when I was eight. There was a dune
of rubbish outside the convent . . . an old sister had died and
they were cleaning out her cell. Big pile of empty chocolate
boxes and biscuit tins . . . Big fat dead nun! I saw this black-
and-white picture, about this size which turned out to be the
lid of a jigsaw box. Two thousand pieces . . . The image was
faded. But the woman on the cover fascinated me. I took it to
teacher. She explained that the woman was an Egyptian
Queen . . . Her name was Nefertiti, meaning 'the perfect one
has arrived'. Graceful neck, impeccable visage. So, I had an
idea. I would repair the royal lady and make a present for
mammy. She was gonna be twenty-five in May. I drew over
the outlines of her features to bring her back to life. I then
made a collage with remnants of yellow velvets and duck-egg
silk . . . but I didn't have any gold fabric. Mam always said it

was bad luck to wear gold . . . so I used Cadbury's foil instead, the bullion wrapper from Tiffin and whole-nut bars. I felt like Big Fat Dead Nun . . . sneaking around for weeks secretly munching. When it was finished, teacher put it on the wall of the class for a whole week and said to the others, 'This and the little girl who made it are really really beautiful.' Jasper smiled at me. I left the room in silence and my heart was Pharaoh purring in my chest. I floated home. That night, I looked at my face for the first time in six long years.

Lispy   If ya live with a cripple, ya copy the Hop.

Her   I should have trusted Lispy Langford . . .

Lispy   If ya live with a cripple, ya copy the Hop.

Her   Heard him gossiping about Jasper and me passin' the staff room.

Lispy   Ooooo, he is one spoilt fucker. From the early minutes of his existence he got whatever his evil little heart screamed out for. Just like his family before him . . . Land-grabbin' Anglo tyrants who fucked the locals off their small farms durin' the famine. Sure they even hosted the Black and Tans in their stables durin' the war. They took and took in the name of British entitlement and they still have it all, the father in his fuckin' blazer leading the mounted pack and now we have his offspring here ensconced . . . You have only to look at the little shit. . . .

Then she speaks sotto voce.

Her   Aldi and Lidl! I knew they hated what they did . . . They admitted that to me, but they had definite plans and were saving hard to get out of debt – loan-shark shit, too long to go inta – and they were trying to send money to their families back home as well. But they never complained about the game. They were trafficked here eight years before, pimped by this Turkish fucker and he had them moved from town to town every three months and it wrecked them. He was involved with heroin as well and got his feet chopped off by a ganglord in Koosadassy and bled to death. So they were free of him at least, and set up shop above me. As independents. Have their own website 'n' all. Customers are regulars mostly . . . And the pervy ones . . . Oh the kinky fella from Wicklow. Fifty shades of Bray!

Jasper   You, O'Sullivan.

We do not see him.

Her   I was walkin' home one Friday, and Jasper called me.

Jasper   You, O'Sullivan!

Her   He was walking five Kerry beagles. Told me he looked up Nefertiti in his encyclopedias. Said she had a gammy eye like me. Said her bust was in a Berlin museum and when Egypt asked for her back, Hitler refused, the fucker. She was trapped cos she was immaculate. Jasper asked me for a loan of money. I gave him two pounds I had from helpin' Mam.

Lispy   Oh, he is one spoilt fucker!

Her   I should have trusted ya, Lispy boy . . .

Lispy (*continues*)   And the world . . . and the world on a platter with machete cutlery so he could hack away chunks of what he wanted and shit away the rest. He walked into this school at the start of September . . . From his scalp to his ankles, just like his father, kicky horse kicky foal . . . like an imperial bastard.

Her   You never know what's around the corner, do ya?

Television   Sofie and Trevor are househunting through the vineyards of Tuscany. We have taken them to an old monastery with super high ceilings and a bellissimo home gymnasium. Ciao, Trevor. Come sta?

Trevor   Bene grazie. I love this place. I love the fitness facilities, the olde-worldy paintings of monks and the proximity to Milan. Sofie is a professional model. We've lost touch with most of our friends. We do have a house that we inherited from Sofie's father, who is dead. Sofie doesn't like to live there any more because she thinks it is haunted, by her late father, who is dead! But, the odyssey continues for me and my sweetheart. Ce bello castello! Is it to your liking, Sofie?

We see him for the third time.

Her Jasper brought me to this grave the July after fifth year. Sat on that slab above and shared a bag of Black Jacks and I kept laughing at his cormorant tongue. He told me that this tomb was actually empty . . . that the remains were exhumed fifty years back . . . a great-great-grand uncle of his who was in the Royal Navy was brought home to England to rest. Horace Wade. Alas, poor Horace . . . I knew nathin' about ya! That Black Jack day . . . he lay on his belly and his arms out like a sphinx. He had a strange-smellin' fag in his mouth. Then, sudden . . . he broke down and told me that he had a sore back. I asked him why. He lifted his shirt and it was raw with veins and white pus. His father drank a bottle of Courvoisier every afternoon at the yacht club and three days before he bate Jasper with a cricket bat when he tried to stop him kickin' the crap out of his mother. She was a total lady and was battered for years by her house-devil husband. She hadn't a tooth left in her head. Poor rich bitch . . .

He disappears. She speaks to his head.

Jasper I'm leaving Saturday night. I'm going to my aunt in Suffolk. I am gettin' the boat from Kingstown.

Her Where?

Jasper Oh, Dun Laoghaire . . . Dublin.

Her How ye gettin' there, Jasper?

Jasper Train. Seven o'clock. Will you wave me off at the station?

Her Of course I will! Of course!

I gave him more money. Five pounds. I didn't ask why. Just stared at his pampas-grass locks and he touched my lips with his thumb.

Sorry, the kinky customer from Wickla. Works for Tesco. Supermarkets . . . fuck! Every month he calls to the girls . . . with his bag for life full of batch loaf, Dairygold and five pairs of heavy denier fashion tights. He strips off, they put the first pair on him and tie him down arms and feet with the other ones. Then they make toast, butter it, spike it on to their stilettos slice by slice and he eats it till he pops! Never lays a hand on them! They taped him the last time on Aldi's phone . . . I nearly pissed laughing when they played it to back . . . 'Feed me toast, gwan, feed me the fuckin' toast . . . D'ya like my tights, feed me the fuckin' toast ya whooerr!' Whaaatttt! Here's a toast to Tesco . . . Every little helps!

Soul-sucking moment number two . . .

Now that's a last breath and a soul headin' home . . .

(*A wispish thought.*) Even before I crossed over, what baffled me was people evading any thoughts of death. I was constantly mulling it through, like would I get a smack of a Volvo, or choke on a Quality Street, would I drown like poor Whitney, God rest her, would I fight for dear life or slip away and surrender. Would I be afraid or kiss the grim reaper. Any of you could be the next corpse. At any moment. What would you most regret not having done? Have a think about that there, now. What would your last words be? I wish I could contact that pizza delivery fella and give him the truth. He is tormented from the cops questioning him every week . . .

I was delighted to leave the house that Saturday evening cos I was overpowered with the stench of bicarbonate of soda! I made a choker from taffeta and a broken-off china cup handle – to remind Jasper that, like the French Emperor, we were just a bone apart! On the way to the station . . . Cobh was spectacular to me like never before.

Mackerel fishers on the dock pullin' in six at a time and the harbour was cobalt below the disk of a tangerine sun. My wrists sweaty with the thrill of seeing him, even if it was gonna be the last time . . . And there he was standing by the quay, where thousands left by tender over the hundreds of years before him. He was timeless in profile, drinking from a flagon with two other lads . . . the Kavanagh girls and Winnie Mattress . . . what were they doin' here? Smoking and skitting laughin'? He smiles my way. The girls skittin' more. The lads whisperin'. But I just blurted it out . . .

It's nearly seven. You'll miss the train

Jasper   What train?

Her   To Dublin.

Jasper   What?

Her   What?

Winnie   What?

Crowd   WHAT?

Her   Have ya a suitcase?

Jasper   What?

Her   What?

Winnie   WHAT? And what's that shit round yer neck?

Her   Stop.

Crowd   STOP.

Her   You said you were leavin'.

Jasper   Leaving?

Crowd   ON A JET PLANE HA HA HA HA HA!

Her   I gave ya money and all.

Jasper   What money?

Winnie   Yeah . . . what money?

Lynchie   Leave her alone, Winnie.

Jasper   Go home.

Her   No, Jasper, you said that your aunt –

Jasper   Go home.

Winnie   Giz a drag, Jasper boy.

Her   But Jasper –

Jasper   I said go home.

Lynchie   Ah, go easy on her, Jasp.

Winnie   Shut up, Lynchee, ya gowl. Go fuckin' home will ya, Sullivan?

Her   No.

Winnie   What ya say.

Her   No I won't, Mattress.

Winnie   What ya call me?

Lynchie   Leave it, Winnie

Winnie   I won't. What you give him money for, ya freak?

Her   I can't believe this is happening.

Winnie   Jasper why she give ya?

Jasper   To kiss her.

Her   What?

Winnie   WHAT? – She looks like a fella!

Her   No!

Jasper   Yes, for weeks . . . so she could have her first ever kisses.

Winnie   You bitch.

Her   This is happening.

Crowd   HA HA HA HA!

Her   That is not true.

Winnie   I don't believe it.

Her   You said your father bate ya –

Jasper   Shut up.

Her   You said he bate ya, and your mother is a punchbag for him.

Jasper   Shut up!

Her   You showed me your wounds.

Crowd   OOOOHHHH!

Her   You said –

Jasper   I said nothin', you varicose bitch. The ugliest bitch I've ever met in my life. You are an example of why animals eat their young. If you played hide-and-seek nobody would look for you. You have a face like a hatful of assholes, you fucking gargoyle.

Her   Stop it!

And I fitted. A colossal one . . . collapsed on the quayside. Out cold. Staggered home somehow . . . Told nobody. Out of school. Mam didn't ask why. Stayed in the house for a year, in the darkness . . . Free from the horror of the tangerine sun.

A small choral sample: 'In all the Earth'.

How do ya know Jesus Christ wasn't from the north side of Cork city? Cos when He fell the first time He didn't put in a claim! All Mam ever told me was that Dad had ran away with a piece of trash from Switzerland. He met her when I was just five and him emptying bins during the folk-dance festival. When I'd ask if he was coming home she would just cry and clean and scrub the house. She got a chronic skin infection and died holding my baby finger in Cobh hospital. I put me communion frock in the coffin beside her. Was that too Stephen King?

Television   Hello everybody. Sofie and Trevor have rejected over six hundred properties in their brutal search for the house of their dreams! Today we have crossed the Mediterranean to North Africa . . . This Tunisian town house boasts a market value of forty pounds and has sixteen rooms . . . After you, Trevor!

Trevor   Immediately, I anticipate a problem. There is no water feature. An oasis is essential to us, really. We don't have any children, per say, as Sofie is allergic, to, am, them . . . but we now have two camels. Sofie is becoming quite the belly-dancer, loves to excavate on her days off and bury herself up to the waist in the sands of Carthage . . . holding her hollyhock-parasol aloft whilst applying her warpaint. Such happy days, aren't they, Sofie?

Her   Anyway, on Mam's first anniversary I sold the house and moved to Cork city. Got work in a hotel kitchen. Night shifts. No one could see me properly, comin' or goin'. I knitted hats and scarfs to cover up with . . . Loved the cold days. Got a bike so I wouldn't have to pass as many so close on the footpath. Godsend. No more fits. The manager was an angel to me, Patchy. Patchy Drizzle he was called. He thought he was an expert on the weather. 'Dare's an anticyclone comin' in from Canada with columbus clouds and spits and spots and lots of patchy drizzle!' He was the loveliest man and always gave me first call on overtime. Kept to meself. Telly, and repairing linen from the hotel as a side earner. At least I could take that home and stitch in front of *Dynasty* and *Tomorrow's World*. A bit of money in the post office for my rainy day and I prayed to Mam to keep things this good . . .

So this woman gets on the bus with her child and the driver says 'Dat's the ugliest baby I ever seen!' So she goes down the

back of the bus all upset and sits beside this ould fella and
she's all crying and 'That is so insulting I can't believe . . . '
and the man says 'What's wrong love' and she says 'I have
never been so affronted in all my . . . ' and he says 'That's
terrible in dis day and age ya poor love . . . If I were you I'd
go back up to that fella and give him a piece of your mind'.
And she goes, 'No, I can't, I am too upset' and he says . . .
'Go on up there and demand an apology, go on, and I'll hold
your monkey!'

*The following with Egyptian style, music and movement . . . much like
the lightning story earlier.*

I was in Cork city seven years. A sweltering second of August
and it was strange for me to be outdoors by day, but I had to
go to Uncle Blaise's funeral, the pet. Dolores was pissed at the
mass but it wasn't in Cobh thank God but Glanmire so I got
the train there and back. After that, up on me bike and down
Panna and that's when I just stopped outside Roches Stores.
And I commanded meself, 'Go in an' buy something girl,
treat yourself.'

So I did. And even though it was roasting, I still had a light
chiffon scarf over me lower face . . . I always wore a veil of
some sort. Not in there two minutes and I saw the brooch, a
glinting owl – cheeky hooters and a gilded beak! I was drawn
to my silly barn owl – Mr Sparkles, that's what I would call
him, and he would perch on my lapel and cheer me through
the winter. Shop was an oven so I took off me scarf to try
him. Delighted with meself and the till-girl let me wear him
out. He just felt right. I was beaming back on the bike.

Cycled the rest of Panna, up the Grand Parade and stopped
at the lights by Finns Corner. The courts were closing on
Washington Street . . . thugs and solicitors all dispersing. Still
at the lights. The heat was Saharan.

He appears.

And then, like a mirage, this legal figure in a black cape and
a white collar came up beside me at the crossing. And my

handlebars went baltic. Then my plexis . . . so cold. It was him . . . and all he did was this.

He gestures, laughs . . . then disappears.

Hand up to me face. No scarf. Fuck it! Left it on the counter. Cycled with every gasp I could take . . . fell outside UCC, cut my hand, blood, people pointing, 'ye alright', bag scattered, coins everywhere, crying, back on the bike, wasp in me hair, nearly hit by a courier . . . Watch the road, ya fuckin' freak beast. The rest is a blank. But I got home. Bandaged my raw palm like a mummy . . . Threw Sparkles in the bin. Small country! I hate owls. I fuckin' hate them.

Knitting . . .

Nearly broke me heart to leave Cork, but, it had to be done. I begged Patchy not to ask me why. Just too painful to explain. And too slow. My stammer was back. He did what I asked and set me up with a job in a Dublin hotel . . . ran by his sister, Bina. She was a tonic. Spina Bina the dubs called her. Story has it that she went to Lourdes as a volunteer in the nineties . . . and out of nowhere she robbed a wheelchair, rolled into the waters . . . then screamed, 'I'm cured, thanks be to holy baby Jesus, I'm cured' . . . got up and walked. Got a huge round of applause and won pilgrim of the week for her being healed from spina bifida! She got a certificate and all . . . it's behind the Reception, framed. Told me she did it just to give all the others hope! Lunatic.

Call and Answer . . . now happy memories.

I loved the girls and they loved me. They got me to go to counselling and it helped me so much. They showed me how to use special cosmetics and do my hair and make an effort. They were all I had and told me that I was holding myself back in life, and would waste it if I did not lose my fears. They took me out on some of their nights off. Even did ballet classes with them. For a year. Good for my posture and confidence, they said. Introduced me to some nice fellas, not customers! I lost my virginity at thirty-five thanks to them.

A steeplejack from Wexford! Tiny! But a long-term lover . . .
just . . . never . . . worked out for me. W' harm.

Television   Sofie and Trevor are ecstatic with joy. After
almost thirty years of searching, they have found their home
of homes here, in the Valley of the Kings . . . Just outside
Luxor, Luxor, Egypt.

Trevor   Sofie has been rendered speechless. We love the
sarcophagus beds. Back of the net! We are surrounded by all
of our worldly goods and have an endless supply of goat's
milk and beer. Sofie is wearing a pet cobra on her head and is
becoming a little bossyboots, ha ha! We are like two perfect
peas in this pyramid pod . . . I love you so much, Sofie. I will
always be your devoted, Trevor!

Sofie glares . . . and whispers . . .

Sofie   No, Antony, Antony!

*She smiles fully and pushes the imaginary block of stone and seals them
both, inside, for ever!*

Then . . .

Her   I know we need beauty, all of us. Need the glimpse of
an exquisite landscape or Venus shimmering in the palm of
the Moon. But I have seen how human beauty works. How
the surface is rewarded above skill. How we flock to be
around the beautiful ones and go out of our way to help
them, how they get promoted faster and forgiven sooner.
How some use it to get exactly what they desire crushing
everybody in their paths. So when was the last time you
judged another . . . just because of this?

Third soul-sucking moment.

For my forty-eighth birthday, twelfth of the third, 'thirteen.
The girls took me clubbing. The best night of my life. The
last night of my life. They teased me to the floor after a
couple of Smirnoffs! All I could see were shapes of others,
their whitest eyes and grills of teeth.

Lights flashing. Dancing like the girl I always wanted to be . . .
soft at the shoulder and hip . . . elegant and free on the waves
of sound . . . rolling on to glassy sand, sinking in the warm
grains and the entire surface of me covered in tiny jewels,
with no stammer, no temper, no disfigurement, no loneliness,
nothing . . . just jewels, dancing.

Her dancing . . . and this ends . . .

Next day, I was a factory. Made new curtains and bought a
bag of paste, a brush and a lovely simple wallpaper to spruce
up the chimney breast for Easter. Raggy ould clothes. The
evening was still dull for March. Had the telly volume mute
and glanced over now and then to see if there was any news
from Rome of the new Papa. Very loud music upstairs from
the girls as they were starting early, fair dues to them. I ran
my cold tap to mix the paste in the basin. Wooden spoon.
Then bell in hall went. I knew the girls wouldn't hear it so I
buzzed the customer in. Routine. More mixing. Swirls.
Knock on my door! Wrong one I'd explain. Tap off. Man
outside coughing. 'Two seconds!' Whuu, heavy cologne.
Open door.

Him. We don't see him . . .

Well, the Perfect One arrives. What are the chances?! There
it is again – that look of disgust at me. Is it because I drew
attention away from ya? Or were ya afraid I was contagious?
Is there a Mrs Wade? Does she know you're paying for it
now? Does the whole of Cork know? And your looks are
slippin' boy. I'd give ya five years and you'll be welcome to
my world . . .

(Stammers.) . . . Ya beautiful empty bastard.

(With tennis sounds.) Play! Door struggle. Bang. Me to the
ground. He's in. Up on me knees. Then his back hand with
the roll of wallpaper. The pain. But I grabs the needles and
stabs him in the wrist. Deuce. The blood spatters. He answers
with a double-strength volly. I fall. No pain. Rise above
meself to an aerial view. See him remain focused . . . tea

towel to block the bleeding . . . Robot clean up . . . forensic
Mr Proper in his Marigolds . . . like Mam. Music still goin'
upstairs . . . white smoke on the TV, wraps me in a curtain
and dash downstairs, checks all clear, slips to the corner,
green bin . . . Merrion Hotel matches – wait – sees a pizza
receipt – pocket – crack and bin in flames – blazing
distraction – back up to me . . . leaves my phone and the
receipt on the draining board. Hauls me up and down and
dumped in the trunk . . . then the bits that are stained
parceled in curtain number two in on top of me. Sneakily
moves off. Black smoke from the green bin. Still above myself
like a Google map . . . through the night . . . past the Curragh
racecourse, Portlaoise, Garda checkpoint at Mitchelstown . . .
waved on! Advantage Jasper. Destination Cobh. Tumbledown
Cemetery. Parks up side lane. Grabs his car jack. Sprints to
Horace's, here. Pumps the slab open with his leg, sprints back
for the stuff and me and STOP! I hear Galapagos on the
main road . . . two a.m. He's older and slower than ever . . .
me shouting with my dead mouth . . . Small country – get the
reg. 09C56 hurry fuckin' up! But he passes by not noticing –
tortoise passes by. Match point. Dragged past Big Fat Dead
Nun and Napoleon's doctor. Bundled in here – car jack down,
grand slam, set and match, Mr Wade.

Sounds of harp continue . . .

I saw Grandad again. I took his hand. And the girls are
baffled that I've disappeared. I see them – utterly puzzled.
Raised the alarm that I'm missing. Admitted to being lap
dancers. Nothin' else – Aldi keeps breaking down. Patchy
came specially to Dublin and put posters all over Baggot
Street with Bina. I'm a cover girl at last.

He gagged me with this. Forgot to take it off me. That haunts
him with his four kids. New mansion near Blarney. One of
the top barristers in the country and he commuting daily
fuelled by vintage cocaine. Still like a Russian doll. Still full of
himself. And his wife is a bakery of make-up cos he bates the
shit out of her but she will grin at his shroud as she is secretly

fucking the redheadfella who sells focaccia in the English market!

Scratching sounds once more.

They're frantic again. It could be a feast of sand crabs. Naw, that's a bird flapping to death . . . I hope it's an owl. Bye, Vicky love. Bring ya a curry chips next time . . . and, thanks for the company, all of ye.

Wind . . . last track begins.

You're sinking, mister . . . to the ebony below. No idea of the massive tumor beside your kidney and it will be a horrible death for ya. So much agony ahead for ya, sir . . . and things goin' wrong. Loadsa tings. But, ye never know what's round the corner, do ya?

A small choral sample: 'How Excellent' and as we began . . . Harps, overlapping, a sucking sound track as the onlooker is whooshed back to reality, and to house lights.

The End.